100 QUESTIONS AND ANSWERS

DISEASES
AND
MEDICINE

Written by
Steve Parker

Edited by
Fiona Mitchell

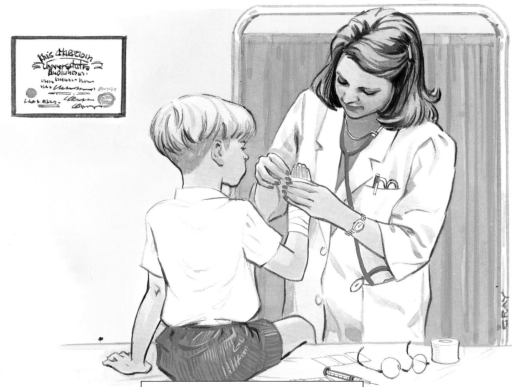

PUFFIN BOOKS

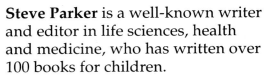

Steve Parker is a well-known writer and editor in life sciences, health and medicine, who has written over 100 books for children.
The consultant, **Ghislaine Lawrence**, is Curator of Clinical Medicine at the Science Museum in London, England.

PUFFIN BOOKS

Published by the Penguin Group
Penguin Books Ltd, 27 Wrights Lane, London W8 5TZ, England
Penguin Books USA Inc., 375 Hudson Street, New York, New York 10014, USA
Penguin Books Australia Ltd, Ringwood, Victoria, Australia
Penguin Books Canada Ltd, 10 Alcorn Avenue, Toronto, Ontario, Canada M4V 3B2
Penguin Books (NZ) Ltd, 182-190 Wairau Road, Auckland 10, New Zealand

Penguin Books Ltd, Registered Offices: Harmondsworth, Middlesex, England

First published 1996
10 9 8 7 6 5 4 3 2 1

Produced for Puffin Books by Zigzag Publishing Ltd, The Barn, Randolph's Farm, Brighton Road, Hurstpierpoint, West Sussex, BN6 9EL, England

Series concept: Tony Potter
Editorial Manager: Hazel Songhurst
Senior Editor: Helen Burnford
Production: Zoë Fawcett and Simon Eaton
Designed by: Ed Org
Illustrations by: Peter Bull, Maureen Gray, Tony Masero
Cover Design: Deborah Chadwick
Cover Illustration: Simon Dewey

Colour separations: RCS Graphics Ltd, Leeds, England
Printed by: Proost, Belgium

Contents

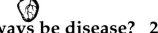

This book answers all your questions about diseases and medicine. It is packed with facts about infections and infestations, the most harmful germs and the rarest diseases, famous doctors and the great medical advances.

Discover the amazing history of medicine and how millions of lives have been saved. Read about the Black Death, "flying doctors" and how animals spread disease.

What were the first diseases? What is alternative medicine? Why did stone-age people have holes drilled in their skulls? Does surgery hurt? You can find the answers to these and many more fascinating questions inside this colourful book.

Fossilized bones show that stone-age people suffered from problems such as arthritis of the joints, and broken bones.

What is disease?

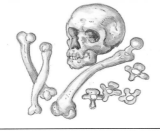

Disease is a sickness which affects the body or mind. There are many different diseases from the common cold to more serious ones that threaten life.

Q Is a runny nose a disease?

A A runny nose is a symptom rather than an actual disease. Symptoms are the effects caused by a disease that people notice or feel. Examples of common symptoms include coughing, stomach pains or aching muscles. A runny nose is usually caused by a viral infection called the common cold. In some cases, however, it might be caused by allergies such as hay fever.

Q What is an infestation?

A An infestation is different from an infection where germs attack the body. An infestation is where parasites or pests live on or in the body. These are usually bigger than germs. They include fleas, lice and ticks on the skin, and tapeworms (pictured below), hookworms and pinworms (threadworms) in the intestines.

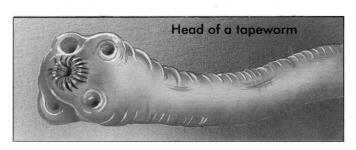

Head of a tapeworm

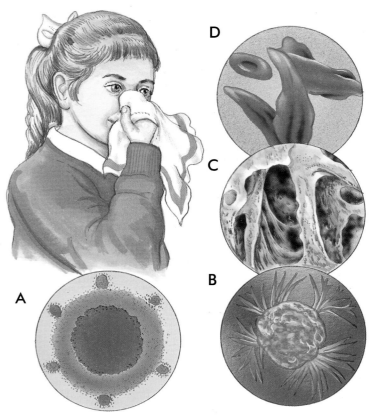

Q What are the main kinds of disease?

A There are many different kinds of diseases. Inflammatory disease (A) can be caused by germs getting into the body and multiplying there. Neoplastic disease (B – cancer) is when some of the body's microscopic cells multiply out of control. Congenital disorders (D) are bodily abnormalities present from birth. Degenerative disease (C – degenerative bone) usually results from old age.

In countries such as Britain and the US, one of the commonest health problems among adults is backache.

Sometimes an illness of the mind can affect the body too. It may cause dizziness, aches and pains, and other problems. This is called a psychosomatic illness.

5

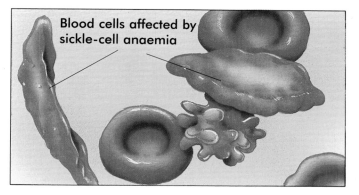

Blood cells affected by sickle-cell anaemia

Q Which diseases last longest?

A Some diseases may last all through life, such as the blood disease called sickle-cell anaemia. It is a severe, hereditary disease which causes round blood cells to become sickle-shaped. Although the disease cannot be cured, doctors may be able to treat the symptoms, so the person does not usually feel ill.

Q Are some illnesses all in the mind?

A Yes. These are called mental or psychiatric illnesses. They are usually based in the brain, and they affect the way a person thinks, acts and behaves. Such illnesses may also have effects on the body, such as trembling or aches and pains. A true mental illness is not "made up" by the sufferer, it is just as real as a physical illness.

Q Which are the rarest diseases?

A There are hundreds of extremely rare diseases, each with only a few sufferers in the world. Severe combined immunodeficiency syndrome (SCIDS) is a disease where the body has no defences against germs. The affected person may have to live in a germ-proof room or plastic tent "bubble".

Q Are some people in perfect health?

A Staying in perfect health is very difficult. The body is always at risk from diseases caused by germs in the surroundings, eating unhealthy foods, putting on too much weight, and even growing old. However, lots of people are mostly healthy throughout their lives.

It was once thought that disease was caused by too much blood. Doctors applied slug-like creatures called leeches to the skin to suck out blood.

What is medicine?

Medicine is the practice of identifying, treating or preventing diseases and illnesses. It has changed vastly through the years and is different all over the world.

Q What is a doctor?

A A doctor is trained to examine people, find out if they are ill, identify the disease, and give treatment to ease suffering and perhaps cure the disease. Modern medicine is very scientific and complicated. Only people who have studied hard and passed all the medical examinations and tests can become qualified medical doctors.

Q Who were the first doctors?

A Even in stone-age times, there were probably people who tried to help others and ease their suffering. One of the first famous doctors was Imhotep of Ancient Egypt, who lived more than 4,600 years ago. He was also a priest, sculptor, pyramid designer, and court official to King Zoser. There were also many doctors in Ancient Greece. Hippocrates of Cos (460-377 BC) is called "The Father of Medicine".

Q Are there more women doctors today?

A More women are becoming doctors. Throughout history most doctors have been men. This was mainly a result of the more powerful position men had in society. Often women were not actually banned, but only men could get full medical qualifications, so only men could lawfully practise medicine.

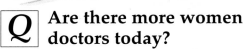

Claudius Galen (130-201 AD) dissected apes to learn about the way in which the human body works.

It takes about five years to qualify as a doctor, whereas becoming a vet – a doctor for animals – takes six or seven years!

Q Did people pray for cures?

A Medicine and healing have long been linked with religion, prayer and worship. Before the work of Hippocrates, most people believed that illnesses were punishments from the gods. People visited temples, said prayers to the gods and left sculptures as offerings.

Q Is a dentist a type of doctor?

A Dentists have the same early training as doctors, then they specialize in their own subject – teeth and gums. Opticians, pharmacists (chemists) and many other health professionals do some medical training in addition to studying their own subject.

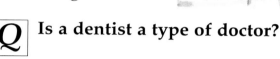

Q What is a nurse?

A A nurse gives general care to sick and ill people, such as washing, feeding and checking body temperature and pulse rate. Carers and nursing helpers have existed since ancient times. The modern nursing profession, with its own training and skills, was developed in the mid 19th century by Florence Nightingale and others.

Q How many kinds of doctors are there?

A In modern medicine, there are many different kinds of doctors. Specialists concentrate on a body part or system. Neurologists, for example, are experts on the brain and nerves while cardiologists specialize in the working of the heart. Other specialists deal with a particular group of people. Paediatricians deal with babies and children. Obstetricians deal with expectant and new mothers and geriatricians with older people.

Acupuncture is used by some doctors for anaesthesia in surgery.

Are there different types of medicine?

Western scientific medicine is used all over the world, but there are many other types of medicine. People around the world view their own kind of medicine as the "normal" one.

Q What is alternative medicine?

A Alternative medicine does not rely solely on drugs or surgery. It has a "holistic" approach to health. This means that the patient's whole body is given treatment, unlike conventional medicine which just treats the part, or system of the body affected. Alternative medicine is practised by people who have a special training in therapies such as homeopathy.

Vital energy flows along channels in the body called meridians.

Q What is acupuncture?

A Acupuncture is an ancient Eastern form of medicine used in countries such as China. It is based on the belief that disease results from disturbances in the way our vital energy or "chi" flows around the body along channels called meridians. Inserting sharp needles into the body at certain points helps to restore the balance and flow of energy, so healing the body.

Q What is aromatherapy?

A Aromatherapy is a type of medicine where oils and lotions are rubbed and massaged into different parts of the body. The oils and lotions have special aromas (scents or smells), usually made from natural products such as flowers and leaves. The aromas and the massage help to relax mind and body, and get rid of stress and illness.

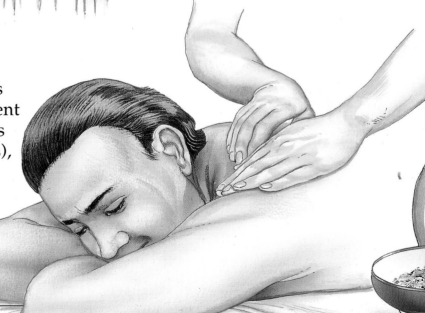

In the 1700s, mesmerism was a popular treatment. It was thought up by Franz Mesmer who claimed to have invisible powers to "cure" the sick.

Radionic therapists claim to be able to diagnose illness by swinging a pendulum above a sample of hair or blood from a patient.

Q **What is reflexology?**

A Reflexology is based on the belief that each part of the body including the brain, heart and other main organs, is represented by a part of the foot. Massaging the feet can help to make the energy or "life force" flow smoothly through the body. This type of medicine was developed in the 1920s by Dr William Fitzgerald and foot-nurse Eunice Ingham.

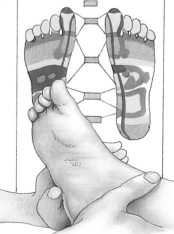

Q **What is herbal medicine?**

A Herbal medicine involves making preparations from herbs, flowers, leaves, roots and other plant parts, to treat sickness and disease. This is one of the oldest forms of medicine, dating back at least 20,000 years. Many modern medicines now manufactured in chemical factories contain ingredients which originally came from plants.

Q **What is homeopathy?**

A Homeopathy uses weak preparations of herbs, minerals and other substances to help treat an illness, when stronger preparations of these substances would cause the same symptoms as the illness. Homeopathy was developed by German physician Samuel Hahnemann, during the early 1800s. His guiding principle was: "Like cures like".

Q **What is hypnotherapy?**

A Hypnotherapy puts someone into a trance to help treat illness and disease. The person in a trance may fall asleep, re-live their memories of childhood or even believe they are someone else. It can help with relief of pain, stress and other problems.

Q **What is chiropractic?**

A This involves manipulating the spine to cure backache and dealing with other damaged joints and bones. It is sometimes claimed that chiropractic can even cure infection. Although there is little evidence that this is true, there is no doubt that chiropractic can help bones and muscular problems.

In Ancient Rome, the scholar Marcus Varro suspected that diseases were caused by "minute creatures which cannot be seen".

What are germs?

Germs are tiny living things that cause illness and disease. Germs are so small that they can only be seen with a microscope. They get into the body in various ways, and breed there, causing infections.

Meningitis bacteria

Pneumonia bacteria

'Flu virus

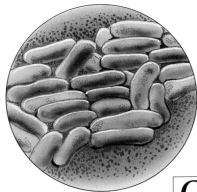
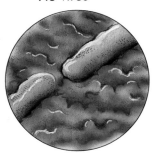

Q Are germs really everywhere?

A Yes, germs are everywhere. They float in the air, and live in dust, soil, water, and the bodies of plants and animals. The most common germs are bacteria and viruses. Bacteria usually measure about 0.001 millimetres across, so you would need 10,000 in a row to stretch to one centimetre.

Q Which are the biggest germs?

A The biggest germs are called the protists (protozoa). Some of them cause infections such as malaria and sleeping sickness (trypanosomiasis). Most protists are about 0.01 to 0.5 millimetres long, so you would need about 1,000 in a row to measure one centimetre.

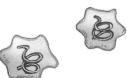

This type of virus causes diseases such as chest and eye infections.

Rabies virus

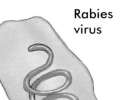

This virus causes respiratory and eye infections.

Q Which are the smallest germs?

A The smallest germs are viruses. Some cause infections such as the common cold, influenza and measles. Viruses are on the borderline between living and non-living things. Some are less than 0.0001 millimetres across. You would need nearly one million in a row to stretch one centimetre.

No one actually saw a germ until the invention of the microscope in 1610.

Some viruses can be turned into powder or crystals, and kept in a bottle for years. When they are put into living tissue they "come alive" again!

Q How are germs killed?

A Chemicals such as antiseptics and disinfectants, and medical drugs called antibiotics, alter the structure of germs or stop them from reproducing. Germs can also be killed using heat. Irradiation is now an important way of sterilising dressings and surgical equipment.

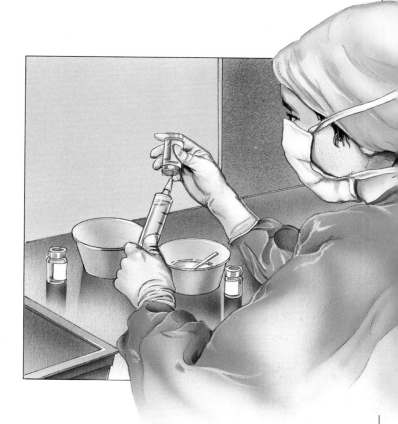

Q How can people prevent germs from spreading?

A Having a bath or shower regularly, keeping clothes clean and washing hands after going to the lavatory prevent germs from spreading. People can make sure that the food they eat and the water they drink is clean. Careful disposal of waste and sewage is very important too.

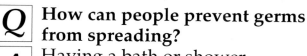

Q Do animals spread germs?

A Flies paddle in rotting food or sewage, then walk on food. Mosquitoes eat germs when they drink people's blood and spread the germs when they bite other people. Fleas and lice do the same. A bite from a wild animal such as a fox can infect the body with germs.

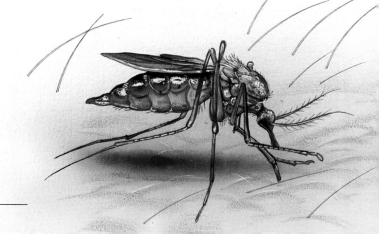

One of the main types of cell which defends you against germs is the white blood cell called the lymphocyte.

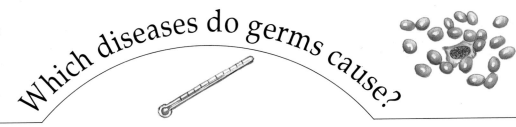

Germs cause the group of diseases known as infections. These range from very mild infections to much more serious ones which can be life threatening.

Q What do germs do in the body?

A They live, grow, multiply and die. This is the germs' way of life, and they are simply doing what comes naturally. Germs can just affect certain body parts such as a part of the skin or mouth. In serious cases, however, germs spread into the bloodstream which leads to septicaemia (blood poisoning).

Q How long do germs live?

A Their lives are usually measured in minutes or hours. Many kinds of bacteria complete their life cycle, from being "born" to splitting into two offspring, in 20 to 30 minutes. This means one bacterium can produce billions within a day.

Salmonella bacteria cause food poisoning when they are eaten in large numbers on contaminated food.

Q How does the body defeat germs?

A The main way is by its immune system. This works against anything which tries to invade the body, from a germ to a splinter of wood. The immune system is based on millions of microscopic cells called white blood cells. They move about the body, eating germs whole, or making natural chemicals such as antibodies that kill or disable the germs.

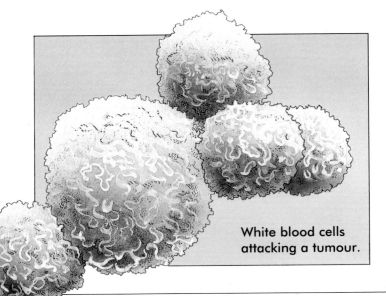

White blood cells attacking a tumour.

An average adult has 1,000,000,000 lymphocytes, weighing the same amount as a bag of sugar.

The largest lymph glands in the body are as big as walnuts. They may swell to the size of apples during an infection.

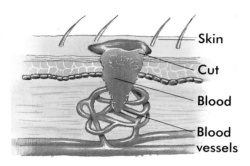

Skin
Cut
Blood
Blood vessels

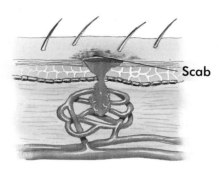

Scab

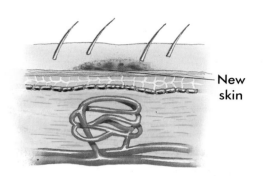

New skin

Q Does your skin prevent infection?

A The skin is the largest organ of your body. It helps to control body temperature, and protects you from infection and injury. If your skin is broken or cut, the blood clots and makes a scab to prevent germs from getting inside your body.

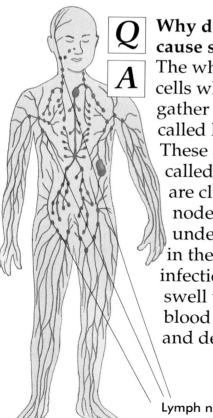

Q Why do some diseases cause swollen glands?

A The white blood cells which fight germs gather in body parts called lymph nodes. These are sometimes called "glands". There are clusters of lymph nodes in the neck, under the armpits and in the groin. During an infection these may swell with extra white blood cells, body fluids and dead germs.

Lymph nodes

Q What is an epidemic?

A An epidemic is when there is "a bug going around" which affects lots of people in one area at about the same time. The "bug" is the germ. Of course there is not one germ, but billions. They thrive and spread due to a combination of factors, such as temperature and weather.

Q Why do some diseases cause a fever?

A A fever is a raised body temperature, from the normal 37°C, to 39°C, 40°C or even more. This is a result of increased chemical activity in the body, due to the battle between its immune defence system and the invading germs.

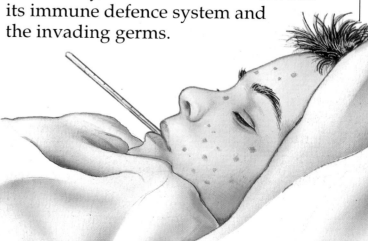

4

How do doctors help?

Doctors are trained to examine people and find out if they are ill. They try to identify the illness, and give advice and treatment to the patient to ease suffering and help recovery.

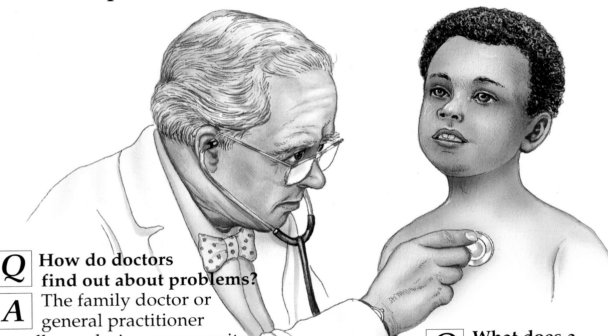

Q How do doctors find out about problems?

A The family doctor or general practitioner usually works in a community. The doctor has medical records for each person who has registered at his or her surgery. These show which diseases and illnesses the person has had in the past, and what happened. The doctor examines the patient, makes a diagnosis which identifies the disease and helps to decide the best treatment.

Q How do doctors reach patients in remote parts of the world?

A In remote parts of Australia and Canada, "Flying Doctors" travel to patients by plane. In Africa, the bush doctor visits patients equipped with a mobile clinic. "Barefoot" doctors in countries such as China are healthcare workers who give simple treatments.

Q What does a stethoscope do?

A A stethoscope is a listening tube, to hear the natural sounds and noises inside the body. These change in certain diseases. The doctor may listen to the thumping of the heartbeat, the swooshing sounds of the lungs breathing, and the digestive gurglings of the stomach and intestines.

Even though medical thermometers were invented in the 1600s, taking the patient's temperature was not thought to be important until at least 200 years later.

In the Middle Ages, doctors diagnosed disease partly by looking at a patient's urine. They would note its colour, cloudiness, frothiness, and taste!

Q Why do doctors look into people's eyes?

A A special instrument called an ophthalmoscope is used for examining the eyes. Inside the eye, the doctor sees tiny, delicate blood vessels and the blood pulsing through them. This can give information about the eye itself, and also the blood system.

Q What are "tests"?

A There are thousands of different medical tests. They help doctors to make an accurate diagnosis of disease. Some tests involve taking a small sample of the body or its products including blood, sputum (spit), urine and pus. The sample goes to a medical laboratory for chemical studies to identify disease. Tests, such as scans, produce detailed images of the human body and so improve diagnosis.

Q What is blood pressure?

A Like water from a tap, the blood is under pressure inside the body's blood vessels. If this pressure gets too high or too low, it can cause various diseases. The doctor measures blood pressure using an inflatable cuff wrapped around the upper arm. This is connected to a U-shaped tube or an electronic meter, called a sphygmomanometer.

Q What is the pulse rate?

A The pulse rate is the speed at which the heart beats. Each heartbeat causes one pulsation throughout the body's system of blood vessels. The pulsation, or pulse, can be felt in a blood vessel in the wrist. Some illnesses make the heart beat speed up or slow down.

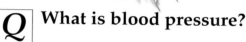
Pulse points

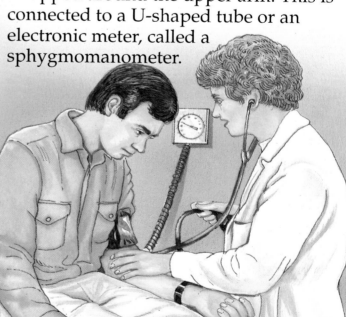

Tooth decay is a common human disease all over the world!

Why are some diseases getting rarer?

Today there are more immunizations (vaccines), well-trained doctors, new drugs and medicines. People in many countries are in better health than ever before.

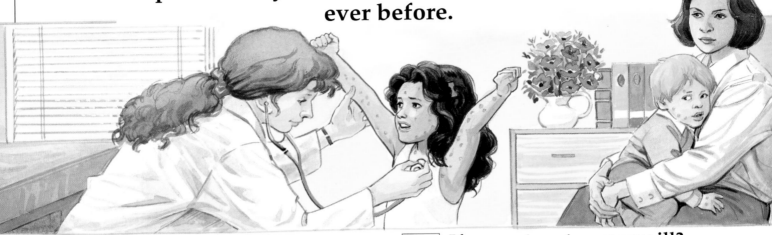

Q Do children have their own illnesses?

A Some infections especially tend to occur in babies and children. They include measles, mumps, rubella (german measles), and chickenpox. Once a person has caught one of these diseases, he or she becomes immune or resistant and is very unlikely to catch it again. Immunizations protect people against getting the disease, even for the first time.

Q If you get spots, are you ill?

A It depends on the type of spot, where it is on the body, and how many there are. Spots can be caused by a general infection such as measles or chickenpox, or by a small patch of infection in the skin, like a boil, or even by the harmful chemicals from a stinging nettle.

Q Can children be born with illnesses?

A Yes. This is known as a congenital illness. It may be a genetic condition such as cystic fibrosis, caused by an abnormal gene inherited from the parents. Some conditions "run in families", like asthma and eczema. This means family members are more likely to develop the illness compared to other people, but no one is certain to suffer from it.

Children used to have operations for conditions such as knock knees or bow legs. Now, doctors wait for a time, because many children naturally grow out of these conditions.

Toxocariasis can cause breathlessness and blindness. It is caused by a tiny worm spread in dog and cat droppings.

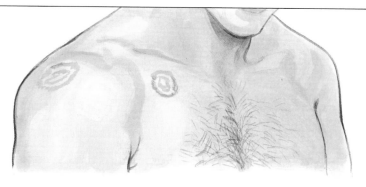

Q How do vaccines work?

A Vaccines or immunizations introduce weakened or dead germs into the body through an injection or on a sugar lump. This prepares the germ-killing cells for attack if active germs invade. In Britain, the dangerous infection called diphtheria used to affect thousands of children each year. Today it is much rarer because of immunization.

Vaccines being tested in a laboratory.

Q What causes a sore throat?

A This is a common symptom, and it has many possible causes. They include a slight infection by viruses or bacteria, a more serious infection such as tonsillitis or diphtheria, or even soreness from shouting too much!

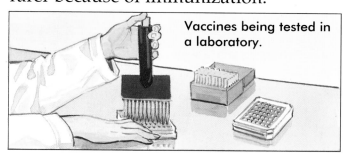

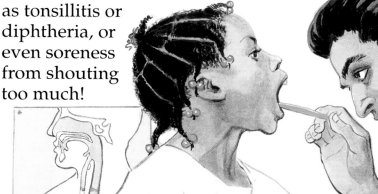

Q Can pets spread disease?

A Yes. Pets are sometimes ill and the germs or other causes can affect humans too, such as worms, bites from fleas on pets and ringworm. Ringworm is not a worm but a type of fungus (mould) growing on the skin. It affects animals and humans.

Q Will you need to stay off school if you are ill?

A This depends on the type of illness. In general, it is not for very long! For common infections such as colds and sore throats, people at school have probably already been exposed to the germs. For a serious infection such as tuberculosis or dysentery, patients are kept on their own. The people who have come into contact with them are traced and seen by doctors.

Before anaethesia, surgery was very painful. Some patients drank lots of wine or beer to get drunk and fall asleep.

Can diseases be cured?

A cure removes the cause of the disease, so that it is unlikely to happen again. This is different to treatment which eases suffering but does not affect the cause of the disease.

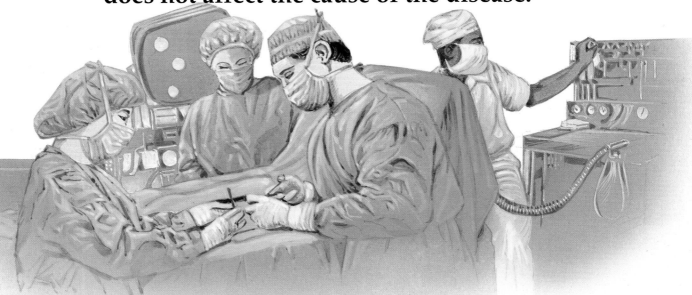

Q What is surgery?

A Originally surgery meant "treatment with the hands" rather than treatment with chemicals or medical drugs. Modern surgery is very safe and involves opening the body to carry out tests, make a diagnosis, or treat a disease. Surgery ranges from quick stitches in a small wound to major organ transplants which can take many hours.

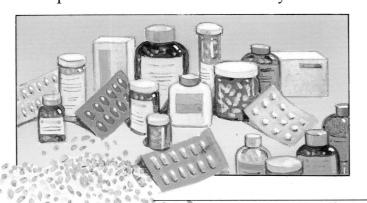

Q Will it hurt?

A Not as much as it used to! Today, there are many ways to reduce pain, such as analgesic (pain-relieving) drugs, and anaesthetics which get rid of feeling and sensation. The first convincing use of anaesthesia was by American dentist-doctor William Morton, in 1846. He used ether gas to put a patient to sleep, while removing a neck tumour (growth).

Q What are medical drugs?

A These are substances (chemicals) that affect the workings of the body and so treat symptoms and cure illness. Thousands of different medical drugs are being invented and tested all the time.

Human skin can now be grown in laboratories to treat people with burns.

Many modern medical drugs are based on natural substances obtained from herbs, plants and animals.

Q What is a prescription?

A Some medical drugs are fairly safe, and people can buy them over the counter from a pharmacist (chemist). Others have powerful effects on the body and can cause problems called side-effects if they are taken in the wrong way. A prescription shows that the doctor advises these kinds of drugs for a certain patient, and explains when and how to take them.

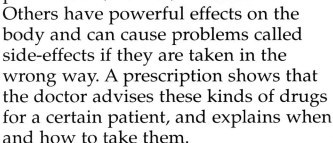

Q What is a scan?

A There are many kinds of medical scanners or imagers. They produce a scan – an image or picture – of the inside of the body, without having to cut it open. Different types of scan show different body parts, such as nerves, blood vessels or abnormal growths. They are used for diagnosis.

Q What are X-rays?

A X-rays are invisible rays that pass through soft body parts, such as muscles and nerves, but not through hard, dense body parts such as cartilage (gristle) and bone. An X-ray photograph, or radiograph, "sees through" the body to detect, for example, broken or abnormally growing bones. X-rays can also be used to treat disease. This is called radiotherapy. However, X-rays must be controlled very carefully as they can be harmful.

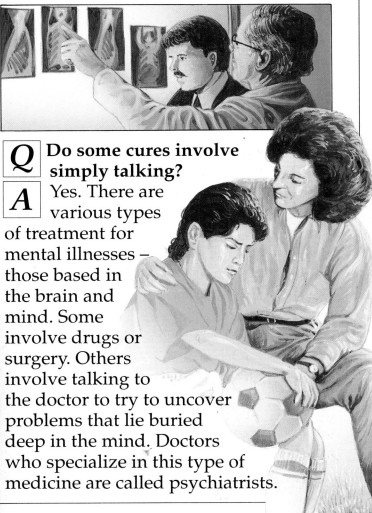

Q Do some cures involve simply talking?

A Yes. There are various types of treatment for mental illnesses – those based in the brain and mind. Some involve drugs or surgery. Others involve talking to the doctor to try to uncover problems that lie buried deep in the mind. Doctors who specialize in this type of medicine are called psychiatrists.

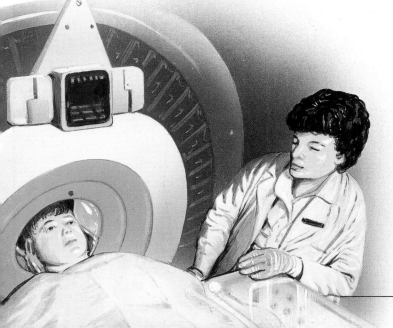

The touch of a king was said to cure tuberculosis. Legend has it that King Charles II cured over 92,000 people in four years.

The "worst" diseases could mean the numbers of people affected, the amount of suffering endured, the length of time people were ill, or the numbers of people killed. Some outbreaks of disease have become world famous.

Q What were the first diseases?

A Bones from stone-age times show that some people had holes in their heads. A sharp stone was drilled or chipped through the skull bone to expose the brain. Some of these patients survived, since the skull bones partly healed again. Perhaps this process, called trepanning, was performed to let out "evil spirits" which were believed to cause illness, but no one really knows.

Q What was the Black Death?

A Bubonic plague is spread by a bacterium, pasteurella pestis, spread by fleas that live on rats and then bite people. One symptom is extremely swollen, painful glands called buboes, in the neck, armpits and groin. The Black Death was a terrible outbreak of the plague which swept across Europe in 1347. It probably killed more than 100 million people.

Q What was the Great Plague?

A The last great outbreak of bubonic plague in Britain was in the 1660s. It killed more than 60,000 Londoners in a few weeks. Large red crosses were painted on the doors of infected households to warn other people of the dangers of infection.

"Ring-a-ring-a-roses, a pocket full of posies, a-tishoo, a-tishoo, we all fall down." This nursery rhyme remembers the flowers that were thought to protect against plague, the sneezing, a symptom, and the likely outcome – death.

When someone in a household caught the plague, the whole family was locked inside for 40 days.

Q Why was smallpox so terrible?

A This terrible viral disease replaced the plague as one of the world's most common and feared illnesses. It produced numerous skin spots (pox) and swellings, which turned into disfiguring sores and ulcers. It could spread into the mouth and windpipe, causing suffocation. It was one of the first diseases to be wiped out by vaccination. Ali Maalin of Somalia caught and recovered from the last known case of smallpox in 1977.

Q How did measles kill millions?

A Measles has been around in Europe for centuries, but many people there have built up bodily immune defences against it. Even as far back as 1490, people in Europe had some natural resistance to measles, but they were carriers of the disease. When they first travelled to the Americas, the native people had no natural defences against measles, and millions of them died. *G34428*

Q What is TB?

A TB or tuberculosis is a bacterial infection that mainly affects the lungs. It was infamous in Ancient Greece, and has been known as consumption or the great white plague. It still affects millions of people around the world, chiefly in warmer countries, and causes tens of thousands of deaths every year.

Q How can 'flu be a mass killer?

A Today when people catch influenza ('flu) they are usually ill for just a few days. In 1918-19, as World War One ended, 'flu spread around the world twice, killing almost 25 million people. This air-filtering mask was believed to help prevent the terrible 'flu.

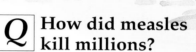

Before the 1900s, experimental blood transfusions were made from animals to humans!

What are the great medical discoveries?

Many people have made medical advances and discoveries through the ages. Their work has helped to ease suffering and save the lives of millions of patients.

Q Who was the first great doctor?

A The first doctor was probably Hippocrates of Ancient Greece, who lived 2,400 years ago. He taught that doctors should give medicines and treatments only when necessary, and make these simple and suitable for the disease. They should keep records so that they could see which treatments were most successful. This was the start of applying science to medicine.

Q How did mouldy bacteria save thousands of wounded soldiers?

A In 1928, Scottish scientist Alexander Fleming experimented with bacteria. Tiny floating spores of a mould landed on the bacteria – and killed them. Fleming named the bacteria-killing chemical penicillin, after the mould which made it, penicillium. It was the first antibiotic drug. Mass produced in the 1940s, it saved many World War Two soldiers, who would have otherwise died from bacteria-infected wounds.

Q Which surgeon did much to help the war wounded?

A French army doctor Ambroise Paré (1517-90) changed surgery throughout Europe. He found that many terrible procedures for wounds, such as pouring boiling oil on them, were unhelpful. It was better to cleanse the wound and bandage it. Paré designed false hands and other body parts, and devised many new operations for eye cataracts and other problems.

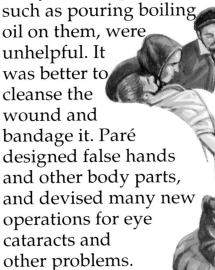

Blood letting (cutting someone to make them bleed) was believed to be a cure for many diseases.

On 3 December 1967, South African surgeon Christiaan Barnard shook the world by putting a dead person's heart into a patient – the first heart transplant.

Q Who suggested simple rather than complicated treatments?

A English physician Thomas Sydenham (1624-89) advised doctors to go back to examining the patient. It was an age when magic, astrology and complicated potions were often part of medical treatments. Sydenham encouraged doctors to treat their patients with simple medication rather than use their patients to test out complicated theories and drugs.

Q Who deliberately gave a boy cowpox?

A In 1796, English country doctor Edward Jenner (1749-1823), infected a boy, James Phipps, with a disease called cowpox – a similar but less serious disease than smallpox. This protected the boy against smallpox. Jenner's work was the beginning of vaccination to protect against infections.

An antiseptic spray used in 1875.

Q Which discoveries opened up a whole new branch of medicine?

A In the 1890s, French scientists Marie Curie and Henri Becquerel discovered that radioactive substances gave off powerful rays. Such rays are today used in the treatment of cancer. This branch of medicine is called radiotherapy.

Q Who made surgery 20 times safer?

A Scottish-born surgeon Joseph Lister (1827-1912) followed the work of French scientist Louis Pasteur, who showed that bacteria caused infections. In the 1860s, Lister used chemicals called antiseptics to kill the germs on his operating instruments and the patient's skin. By the end of the century, surgery was a lot safer.

Malnutrition is caused by poor diet. It can also be the result of anorexia nervosa where people wrongly believe that they are overweight.

There are lots of reasons. They vary from the climate, traditional lifestyles, eating habits, the amount of money available for medical care, and the way people are educated about health, hygiene and cleanliness.

River blindness is caused by flies in Central Africa. It can be detected by examining the skin for lumps.

Q Does the weather affect diseases?

A Yes. Germs, worms and other parasites, and disease-spreaders such as flies and mosquitoes thrive in warm, moist conditions, such as tropical rainforests. They cause diseases such as malaria and sleeping sickness. The diseases of cooler places such as Europe and North America vary in origin and are often related to lifestyle.

Q Is what you eat important?

A Yes. Lack of good food means the body cannot stay healthy and fit. It becomes more susceptible to diseases of all kinds. Malnutrition can be lack of sufficient food, and also lack of food variety. It is perhaps the greatest single factor in the world that contributes to disease. In severe cases it can lead to death. In 1984, a drought in Ethopia led to widespread famine. Many people died.

Q Can disease be caused by living conditions?

A Cramped, damp living conditions encourage infections to spread. Inadequate disposal of waste and sewage and unclean water for drinking, cooking and washing also encourage illness.

In the 1940s-50s, it was fashionable to smoke cigarettes. Now that the severe dangers of tobacco are known, smoking has become much less popular.

It is thought that on average, every cigarette that a person smokes takes 6 minutes off his or her life.

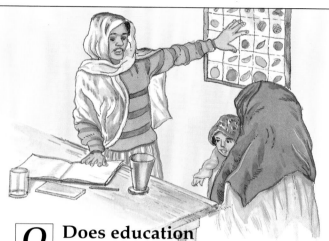

Q Does education affect disease?

A If people learn about health, hygiene and medicine, and about germs and how illnesses happen, then they are more able to prevent diseases, and treat them when they occur. Health education informs people about the importance of a varied diet, cleanliness and caring for children.

Q Which diseases affect rich countries more?

A In general, illness and disease are more common in poor countries but richer countries have diseases too. These are sometimes the result of unhealthy diets and a lack of exercise. They are called "diseases of excess" and include various heart and blood-vessel conditions. Problems such as arthritis and breathing difficulties can stem from being overweight.

Q Does pollution cause disease?

A Many factories produce smoke which lingers in the air as smog. This has been connected to problems such as cancer and respiratory diseases. However, "clean air acts" have improved air quality in London, UK and Tokyo, Japan, and many other cities. In the past, factory waste was also a cause of water pollution. This health hazard has been virtually wiped out due to safer waste disposal.

Protective clothing makes it possible for human beings to work safely in dangerous conditions.

Q Do working conditions affect disease?

A Sometimes. Many countries have rules and regulations about workplaces, to lessen the risks of being injured or causing illness. In some countries, there are fewer regulations. People may get ill through breathing dangerous dust or fumes, handling poisonous chemicals or straining their bodies too hard.

Do new diseases appear?

Germs evolve and sometimes change slightly so that they become more harmful. New diseases such as AIDS and different forms of cancer have appeared.

Q What is HIV?

A HIV is the virus which causes the syndrome known as AIDS. HIV means Human Immunodeficiency Virus. This virus affects the human immune system and damages it. This means the immune system can no longer protect the body against germs and illness.

Q What is HIV-positive?

A It means that a person has had a test to detect HIV in his or her body, and the test is positive – which means HIV is present. It is generally thought that around 50 per cent of HIV-positive people will develop AIDS within ten years. The HIV test does not detect the virus itself. It detects the body's natural chemicals called antibodies which are made to combat the virus.

Q What is AIDS?

A Acquired Immune Deficiency Syndrome (AIDS) is the illness caused by the virus HIV. Symptoms of the illness are many and varied. They include skin growths and greater risk of infections such as pneumonia and tuberculosis. They may not develop for many years after the person first becomes infected with HIV. No one has yet recovered from AIDS.

Q How can HIV infection be prevented?

A The virus is spread by the "exchange of blood or body fluids". This may occur when infected people have unprotected sex or when people who use drugs share needles. Avoiding these reduces the risk of catching HIV. If a mother has HIV, she may pass it to her baby at birth. Much research is being carried out to find a vaccine that will protect against HIV.

HIV viruses are tiny. More than 200 million would fit on the full stop at the end of this sentence.

In diseases such as cancer, a person is only considered cured when the cancer does not return after five years.

Q What is cancer?

A Although the word "cancer" has been around since Ancient Greece, it has only been understood in the modern sense of the word since the late 1800s. Cancer is when malignant cells form a swelling or tumour which spreads and damages other cells. Some cancers remain in one area of the body, while others spread throughout the body by making their way into the blood system.

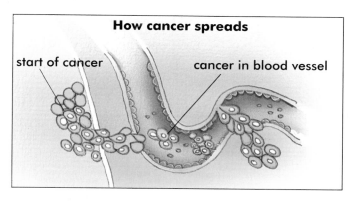

How cancer spreads

start of cancer

cancer in blood vessel

Q How is cancer treated?

A Cancer can be treated in several ways. Surgery can be used to remove the cancer. X-rays can be used to kill cancer cells in a form of treatment known as radiotherapy. The treatment known as chemotherapy uses drugs which are toxic (poisonous) to destroy cancer cells.

Q What kinds of cancer are more common today?

A There are many different kinds of cancer. Some cancers are becoming more common while other kinds are getting rarer. For example, according to modern medical records, lung cancer has become much more common today, reflecting the number of people who started smoking up to 40 years ago.

Q Can cancer be cured?

A Many kinds of cancer can be treated more effectively than ever before, and more kinds can be cured too. One important factor is detecting the cancer in its early stages, which gives a better chance of treatment or cure. The likelihood of being cured is high for certain types of cancers that affect children, such as childhood leukaemia, which affects the white blood cells.

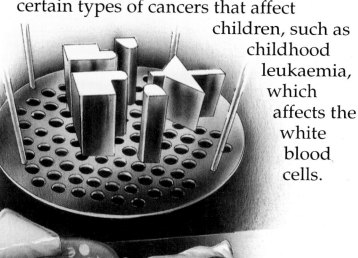

Malaria is one of the earliest recorded diseases. It still kills up to two million people each year.

Will there always be disease?

Over the centuries, people in many parts of the world have become healthier. Yet new diseases appear and as more people live longer, illnesses of the ageing body also increase.

Q Are people healthier today?

A According to sparse and scattered historical records, in the past most people had at least one disease and some people had lots. Proper medical records have only been kept in recent times, and even then, not in all countries. They show a general trend towards a higher proportion of healthy people, and fewer diseases.

Q Did people die younger in the past?

A Yes. During the Middle Ages in Europe, people lived for about 30 years on average. In fact, huge numbers of babies died before their first birthday. New mothers were also at great risk. The improvement of medical care in pregnancy, childbirth and early infancy has greatly helped to increase the average lifespan to over 70 years in Europe today.

Q Are children healthier today?

A Yes. One of the main reasons is immunization. Around the world mass immunization programmes have protected millions of babies and children against dreaded diseases such as polio, tetanus and measles. Researchers are now working on an immunization against malaria.

Q Has life expectancy increased all over the world?

A Life expectancy is increasing in almost all countries of the world. However, war and natural disasters such as earthquakes and floods are responsible for the deaths of millions of people.

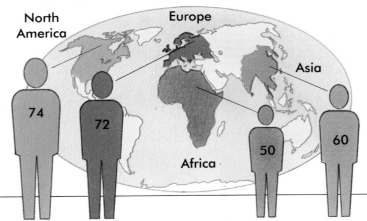

North America 74

Europe 72

Asia 60

Africa 50

Q Can people make new germs to cause new infectious diseases?

A Scientists can make new germs by the process of genetic engineering. New germs are being tested for various purposes, such as rotting plastics and recycling sewage more effectively. In theory, new diseases could be made in a similar way, but there are many laws surrounding genetic engineering which should prevent this.

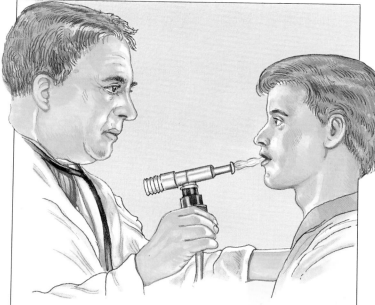

A virus containing the correct gene is sprayed into the lungs of a person suffering from the genetic disease cystic fibrosis.

Q Can people be brought back to life?

A Some people believe that medical science will one day be able to bring people back to life and cure all illnesses. They ask for their bodies to be frozen after death in the hope that one day they will be defrosted and cured of the illness that killed them. This process is called cryonics.

Q Is there a cure for congenital disease?

A Some congenital diseases are caused by abnormal genes. In some cases gene therapy can identify and replace faulty genes. In principle, correct genes can be attached to a harmless virus which is injected into the body and so correct the fault.

30

People who are HIV-positive often feel healthy until they begin to develop AIDS.

How can I stay healthy?

Health comes from the old English word *haelth* meaning whole. It is the excellent functioning of the body and mind. Almost everyone can do something to improve their health, get fit, prevent illness and avoid disease.

Q What is a healthy lifestyle?

A A healthy lifestyle involves taking care of yourself – your body and mind.
- Eat varied, healthy foods, especially fresh fruits and vegetables.
- Do not get overweight or smoke.
- Keep fit by staying active and taking exercise.
- Avoid stress and worrying about things.
- Make sure that you relax occasionally and that you have enough sleep.
- Listen to what your doctor says.

Q Are check-ups important?

A Yes. They are designed to detect diseases which people may be unaware of. Sometimes diseases have no symptoms in the early stages, but can be identified by simple tests. There are dozens of different tests and check-ups, but they are not given to everyone. Many check-ups are designed for particular groups of people, like babies or older people. These are called the target groups.

Q Is sleep important?

A Sleep is very important because it allows your body to build up the energy that it has used throughout the day. You spend about a third of your life asleep. If you did not sleep for about two weeks you might go mad or even die!

Q Should I ignore health problems?

A As soon as you notice a health problem, you should tell an adult. If they think it is important, they will probably make an appointment for you to visit a doctor or medical person. Many illnesses can be treated and cured if detected in their early stages.

About 70% of your body is water. An adult loses 2 to 3 litres a day. This must be replaced by drinking and eating watery foods.

Over 10% of body tissue is made of protein. Protein is an essential part of the diet.

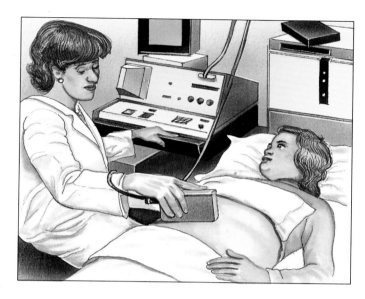

Q **What are the first check-ups people ever have?**

A They begin even before a child is born! The doctor or midwife checks expectant mothers and their unborn babies. These pregnancy checks often include ultrasound scans to enable doctors to check the baby's progress. Newborn babies have several check-ups, and their size and weight are measured. The check-ups are often combined with immunizations.

Q **Can medicine do harm as well as good?**

A Medicine is not harmful if it is carried out properly. Medical drugs are sometimes misused or abused. Illegal drug-taking is very dangerous. Drug addicts suffer from mental and physical side effects which can kill them. Drug addiction can also lead to homelessness and a criminal record.

Q **What are other common check-ups?**

A Throughout life, people should go to the dentist for dental checks, and, if they have a sight problem, to the optician or ophthalmologist for eye checks. Many middle-aged and older people have a general check-up every year or so to test blood pressure and the heart and lungs. After a certain age, women are advised to have check-ups to detect cancer.

Q **What are home testing kits?**

A Special kits are available from pharmacies for checking blood pressure, blood sugar levels or cholesterol, a fatty substance in the blood. Home-testing kits can be used by diabetics to monitor their condition and so improve control of the disease.

Index

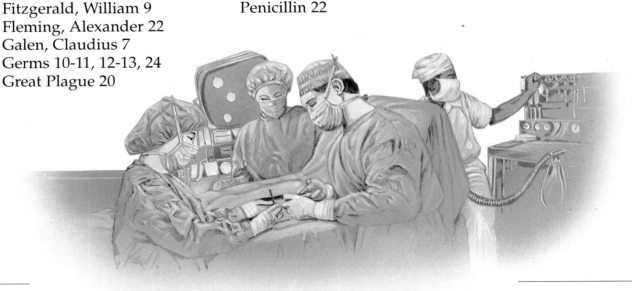